Choose Joy

A COLORING BOOK OF GRATITUDE AND WONDER

Ink &
Willow

Trade Paperback ISBN 978-0-593-23220-0

COLOR YOUR WAY TO GRATITUDE AND WONDER

Choose joy. Gratitude. Wonder.

These are all words and phrases we throw around flippantly. We hand-letter them onto canvases and stick them on our walls. We make graphics of them and post them to Instagram. We get them tattooed on our wrists.

But when we turn on the news, when we get that diagnosis, when we say good-bye to a loved one or lose that job, those words seem to deflate right out of our vocabulary and hearts entirely.

There are many reasons to be worried, upset, and sad these days. It's easy to watch the news and feel overcome with fear, dread, and anger. With political strife, pandemics, wars, and much more dominating the news, the idea of choosing joy as we rest in gratitude and wonder of the blessings around us feels like quite the empty gesture. But that is precisely what we as people of faith are called to do.

When we feel overwhelmed by the pain, suffering, and injustice in the world we cannot personally fix, pausing to stand in gratitude and wonder of our amazing God reminds us that indeed we aren't in control—and thank goodness for that. The same God who created the beautiful trees swaying gently in the wind in your front yard, the same God who created your children, your friends, and your family, the same God who made everything good and beautiful in this world is in control. Taking the time to choose joy as we meditate on gratitude and the wonder of our awesome God is the best way for us to realize that while we might not be big enough to fix our broken world, our God is.

Finding the time to slow down our hectic lives long enough to revel in that gratitude and peace is hard to do. That is why this book exists. Within these pages, you'll find words from writers, teachers, preachers, and the Scriptures that will remind you of the wonder of our awesome God. As you break out your favorite art supplies to color these pages, we hope you meditate on the words written on the page to remember how blessed we are, and what a big God we serve.

Consider this your official invitation to let go. Let go of your need to control things you couldn't control in the first place. Let go of the illusion that you can fix our unwell earth. Choose to sit in joy, gratitude, and wonder. Use these pages to help you slow down and remember what God has done for you and what He continues to do. At the back of the book, you'll find the link to a Spotify playlist that we hope will help amplify your time with this book and usher you into a more complete moment of worship and gratitude.

So go ahead, take a few minutes out of your busy day, let your soul relax, and choose joy. And if you'd like to share some of your artwork and engage with other people using this book, post it on Instagram using the hashtag #ChooseJoyColoringBook.

FiLL the earth with your Songs of GRATITUDE

CHARLES SPURGEON

When the winter is past, and the rain is over and gone,
fill the earth with your songs of gratitude. But remember,
O Believer, that you should sing your Well-Beloved a song
chiefly when it is not so with you, when sorrows befall.

—Charles Haddon Spurgeon, in a sermon delivered at the
Metropolitan Tabernacle in Newington, London, on March 5, 1871

Illustrated by Ann-Margret Hovsepian

COUNT your BLESSINGS, name them ONE by ONE

JOHNSON OATMAN JR.

Count Your Blessings

When upon life's billows you are tempest tossed,
When you are discouraged, thinking all is lost,
Count your many blessings, name them one by one,
And it will surprise you what the Lord hath done.

REFRAIN:
Count your blessings, name them one by one;
Count your blessings, see what God hath done;
Count your blessings, name them one by one;
Count your many blessings, see what God hath done.

Are you ever burdened with a load of care?
Does the cross seem heavy you are called to bear?

Count your many blessings, ev'ry doubt will fly,
And you will be singing as the days go by. [Refrain]

When you look at others with their lands and gold,
Think that Christ has promised you His wealth untold;
Count your many blessings, money cannot buy
Your reward in heaven, nor your home on high.
[Refrain]

So, amid the conflict, whether great or small,
Do not be discouraged, God is over all;
Count your many blessings, angels will attend,
Help and comfort give you to your journey's end.

—Johnson Oatman Jr. (1856–1922) was not a good singer, but at age thirty-six he discovered a different musical talent: songwriting. By the end of his life, Oatman had penned more than five thousand songs. He wrote "Count Your Blessings" in 1897, and though it wasn't one of his personal favorites, it would become one of his most famous.

Illustrated by Katie Howe
Hand-lettered by Ann-Margret Hovsepian

Reflect upon your present blessings—of which every man has many—not on your past misfortunes, of which all men have some.

—Charles Dickens, from A Christmas Dinner, *a short story written in 1835 by the young author about a charming celebration at the home of his Uncle George.*

Illustrated by Laura Marshall Denny

To live with joy
is to live with
wonder
gratitude
and
hope

—David Brooks

Happiness fades; we get used to the things
that used to make us happy. Joy doesn't fade.
To live with joy is to live with wonder, gratitude, and hope.

— *David Brooks, from* The Second Mountain: A Quest for a Moral Life
(Random House, 2019). Brooks, a New York Times *bestselling author,
is considered one of America's leading writers and commentators.*

Illustrated by Holly Camp

Gratitude is an offering precious in the sight of God,
and it is one that the poorest of us can make
and not be poorer but richer for having made it.

—A. W. Tozer, in The Set of the Sail: Spiritual Guidance for the Christian Life
(Moody, 1986). What Tozer (1897–1963) heard from God,
he delivered through sermons and books.

Illustrated by Jennifer Tucker

Love CASTS OUT FEAR, AND *gratitude* CAN CONQUER PRIDE

Louisa May Alcott

Love casts out fear, and gratitude can conquer pride.

—Louisa May Alcott, in Little Women. Alcott (1832–1888) originally published the novel in two volumes in 1868 and 1869 at her publisher's request.

Illustrated by Bridget Hurley
Hand-lettered by Ann-Margret Hovsepian.

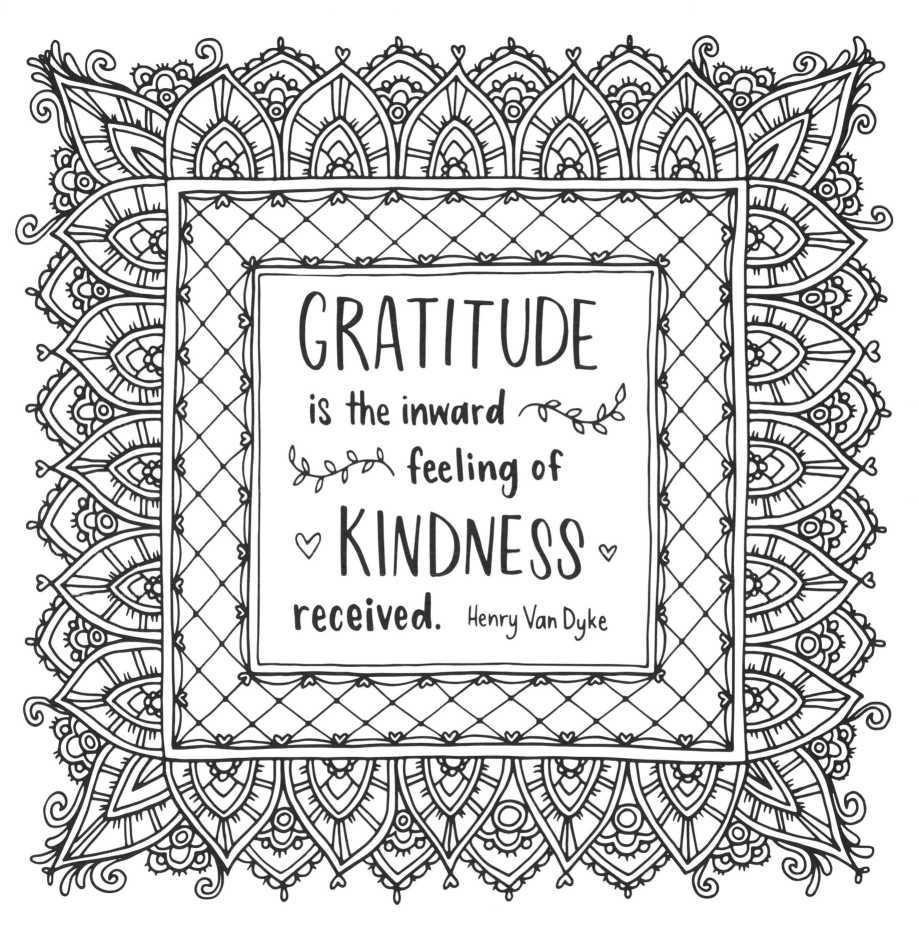

Gratitude is the inward feeling of kindness received.
Thankfulness is the natural impulse to express that feeling.
Thanksgiving is the following of that impulse.

—Henry van Dyke, an American author, educator, and clergyman, in the early 1900s

Illustrated by Ann-Margret Hovsepian

Sing to the LORD with thanksgiving.

—*Psalm 147:7*

Illustrated by Jennifer Tucker

All Will Be Well

Through the love of God our Savior,
All will be well;
Free and changeless is His favor;
All, all is well.
Precious is the blood that healed us;
Perfect is the grace that sealed us;
Strong the hand stretched out to shield us;
All must be well.

Though we pass through tribulation,
All will be well;
Ours is such a full salvation;
All, all is well.

Happy still in God confiding,
Fruitful, if in Christ abiding,
Holy through the Spirit's guiding,
All must be well.

We expect a bright tomorrow;
All will be well;
Faith can sing through days of sorrow,
All, all is well.
On our Father's love relying,
Jesus every need supplying,
Or in living, or in dying,
All must be well.

—Mary Bowley Peters (1813–1856) was a British hymn writer who wrote
more than fifty by the time she was thirty.

Illustrated by Katie Howe
Hand-lettered by Ann-Margret Hovsepian

It's not so much what we have in this life that matters,
it's what we do with what we have.

—Fred Rogers (1928–2003), better known to millions as Mister Rogers, was the host of the
preschool television series Mister Rogers' Neighborhood from 1968 to 2001.
Mister Rogers, who dedicated his life to understanding children, was also a minister.

Illustrated by Laura Marshall Denny

This is a wonderful day. I've never seen this one before.

— Maya Angelou, from her tweet on May 17, 2013. Born Marguerite Annie Johnson, Dr. Maya Angelou (1928–2014) was a respected and award-winning writer, poet, and civil rights activist. She was the first black woman to write a screenplay for a major film release.

Illustrated by Jennifer Tucker

Gratitude is thanking God after it happens.

Faith is thanking God before it happens.

—Mark Batterson

Gratitude is thanking God after it happens.
Faith is thanking God before it happens.

—Mark Batterson, from his tweet on March 31, 2015.
Batterson is a pastor and New York Times bestselling author.

Illustrated by Holly Camp

Even though we face the difficulties of today and tomorrow, I still have a DREAM

MARTIN LUTHER KING JR.

Even though we face the difficulties of today and tomorrow,
I still have a dream.

I would maintain that thanks are the highest form of thought;
and that gratitude is happiness doubled by wonder.

—G. K. Chesterton, in A Short History of England, 1917. An English essayist, Chesterton (1874–1936) wrote more than 100 books, ranging from novels to Christian apologetics.

Illustrated by Ann-Margret Hovsepian

Every good and perfect gift is from above, coming down from the Father of the heavenly lights, who does not change like shifting shadows.

—James 1:17 (NIV)

Illustrated by Jennifer Tucker

Be thankful in all circumstances, for this is God's will
for you who belong to Christ Jesus.

—1 Thessalonians 5:18 (NLT)

Illustrated by Katie Howe
Hand-lettered by Ann-Margret Hovsepian

Praise God from Whom All
Blessings Flow

Praise God, from whom all blessings flow;
Praise Him, all creatures here below;
Praise Him above, ye heav'nly host;
Praise Father, Son, and Holy Ghost.
Amen.

—Thomas Ken (1637–1711) was an Anglican bishop and hymn writer. In 1673, he wrote three hymns for students at Winchester College that he wanted them to sing daily. Each of these closed with these four familiar lines we now know as the Doxology.

Illustrated by Laura Marshall Denny

Gratitude begins

where our sense
of entitlement ends

— Steven Furtick

When entitlement is high, gratitude is low.
When gratitude is high, entitlement is low.
Gratitude begins where our sense of entitlement ends.

— Steven Furtick, from Crash the Chatterbox *(Multnomah, 2014).*
Furtick is a pastor and New York Times *bestselling author.*

Illustrated by Holly Camp

It is not how much we have, but how much we enjoy, that makes happiness. There is more sweet in a spoonful of sugar than a cask of vinegar. It is not the quantity of our goods, but the blessing of God on what we have, that makes us truly rich.

—*Charles Haddon Spurgeon, in* John Ploughman's Pictures: Or, More of His Plain Talk for Plain People *(Farm and Fireside Co., 1881). Spurgeon (1834–1892), known as the "Prince of Preachers," was one of the most influential preachers of his day.*

Illustrated by Jennifer Tucker

FILL YOUR LIFE WITH GRATITUDE AND YOU'LL SPILL OVER WITH LOVE

- BOB GOFF -

Fill your life with gratitude and you'll spill over with love.

— Bob Goff, from Live in Grace, Walk in Love: A 365-Day Journey.
Goff, a former attorney, is a New York Times bestselling
author and encourager to millions.

Illustrated by Bridget Hurley
Hand-lettered by Ann-Margret Hovsepian

Gratitude is the fairest blossom that springs from the soul.

—Henry Ward Beecher (1813–1987), an influential American preacher and supporter of the abolition of slavery, was the brother of author Harriet Beecher Stowe.

Let them praise the LORD for his great love
and for the wonderful things he has done for them.
For he satisfies the thirsty
and fills the hungry with good things.

—Psalm 107: 8–9 (NLT)

Illustrated by Jennifer Tucker

gratitude PRODUCES DEEP, *abiding* JOY

CHARLES STANLEY

Gratitude produces deep, abiding joy because we know
that God is working in us, even through difficulties.

— Charles Stanley, from Sermon Notes (SN111120) for
"Overflowing with Gratitude" (In Touch Ministries, 2015)

Illustrated by Katie Howe
Hand-lettered by Ann-Margret Hovsepian

It is only with gratitude that life becomes rich

Dietrich Bonhoeffer

In ordinary life, we hardly realize that we receive a great deal more than we give, and that it is only with gratitude that life becomes rich.

—*Dietrich Bonhoeffer penned these words from a prison cell in a letter to his parents in September 1943. Bonhoeffer, a German pastor who tried to help Jews escape Nazi oppression, was executed by the Nazis in 1945 for his part in a plot to overthrow Hitler.*

Illustrated by Laura Marshall Denny

God doesn't want us to just feel gratitude, but for us to show it by *giving thanks*

~ R. C. Sproul

God doesn't want us to just feel gratitude, but for us to show it by giving thanks to God with our lives.

— R. C. Sproul, from his tweet on November 23, 2017. A pastor, theologian, and prolific author, Robert Charles Sproul (1917–2017) was the founder and chairman of Ligonier Ministries.

Illustrated by Holly Camp

God is in control, and therefore in EVERYTHING I can give thanks—not because of the situation but because of the One who directs and rules over it.

—Kay Arthur, in As Silver Refined: Answers to Life's Disappointments (WaterBrook, 1997). Arthur is an international Bible teacher whose passion is that every believer in Christ would live out God's Word every day.

Illustrated by Jennifer Tucker

I will give thanks to the LORD with my whole heart;
I will recount all of your wonderful deeds.

—*Psalm 9:1*

Illustrated by Bridget Hurley
Hand-lettered by Ann-Margret Hovsepian

When life is sweet, say thank you and celebrate.
And when life is bitter, say thank you and grow.

—*Shauna Niequist, in* Bittersweet: Thoughts on Change, Grace,
and Learning the Hard Way *(Zondervan, 2013)*

Illustrated by Ann-Margret Hovsepian

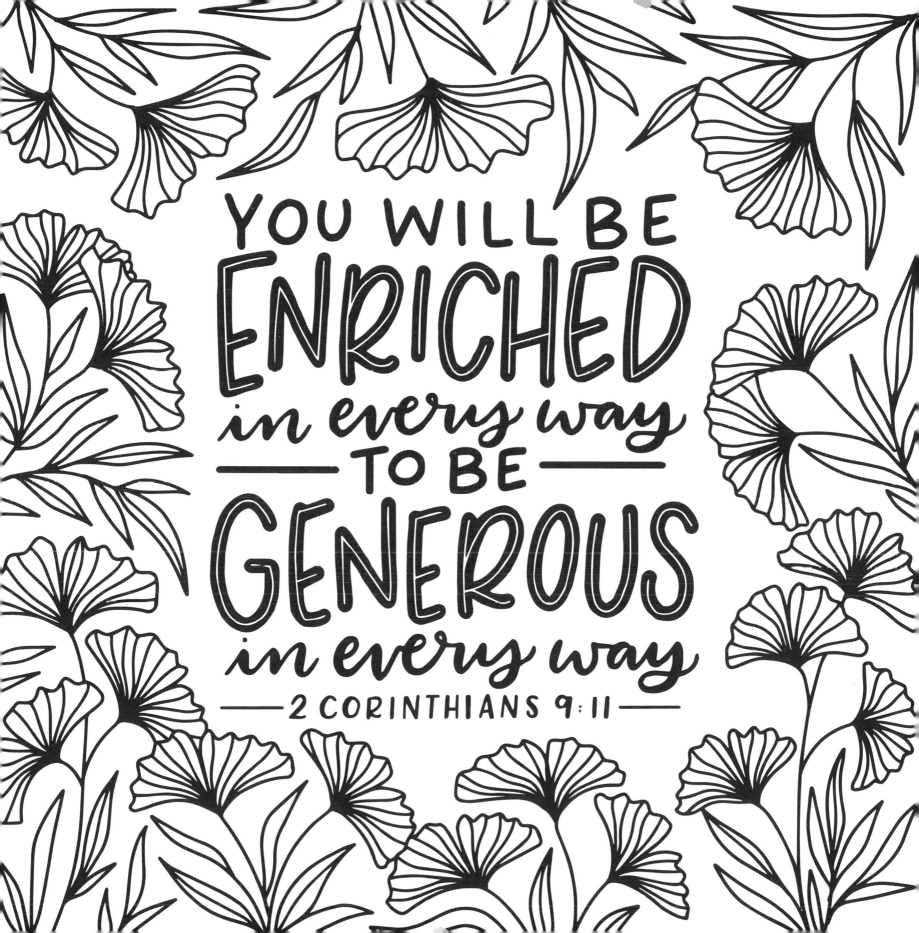

You will be enriched in every way to be generous in every way,
which through us will produce thanksgiving to God.

—*2 Corinthians 9:11*

Illustrated by Jennifer Tucker

Wonderful Peace

Far away in the depths of my spirit tonight
Rolls a melody sweeter than psalm;
In celestial-like strains it unceasingly falls
O'er my soul like an infinite calm.

REFRAIN:
  Peace, peace, wonderful peace,
  Coming down from the Father above!
  Sweep over my spirit forever, I pray
  In fathomless billows of love!

What a treasure I have in this wonderful peace,
Buried deep in the heart of my soul,
So secure that no power can mine it away,
While the years of eternity roll!

I am resting tonight in this wonderful peace,
Resting sweetly in Jesus' control;
For I'm kept from all danger by night and by day,
And His glory is flooding my soul!

And I think when I rise to that city of peace,
Where the Author of peace I shall see,
That one strain of the song which the ransomed will sing
In that heavenly kingdom will be:

Ah soul, are you here without comfort and rest,
Marching down the rough pathway of time?
Make Jesus your friend ere the shadows grow dark;
Oh, accept this sweet peace so sublime!

—*Warren Donald Cornell (1858–1936) was a Methodist preacher
in Berlin, Wisconsin, when he wrote this hymn in 1889.*

*Illustrated by Katie Howe
Hand-lettered by Ann-Margret Hovsepian*

Every time we decide to be grateful it will be easier to see new things to be grateful for

HENRI NOUWEN

Every time we decide to be grateful it will be easier to see new
things to be grateful for. Gratitude begets gratitude,
just as love begets love.

—Henri J.M. Nouwen, in Life of the Beloved: Spiritual Living in a Secular World
(Crossroad, 1992). The world-renowned Dutch author, priest, and professor dedicated
his life to the spiritual values of communion, community, and ministry.

Illustrated by Laura Marshall Denny

Thank God for all He does for us which we do not deserve.

– Billy Graham

Even when life may be difficult, we should thank God for all
He does for us which we do not deserve.

—*Billy Graham, in* Answers to Life's Problems: Guidance, Inspiration, and Hope for
the Challenges of Today *(Thomas Nelson, 1997). Graham (1918–2018) was an evangelist
who is considered to be among the most influential Christian leaders of the twentieth century.*

Illustrated by Holly Camp

To be GRATEFUL is to recognize the LOVE of GOD in everything HE HAS GIVEN US— and He has given us EVERYTHING

- THOMAS MERTON

To be grateful is to recognize the Love of God in everything
He has given us—and He has given us everything.

—*Thomas Merton, in* Thoughts in Solitude *(Farrar, Straus and Giroux, 1999).
Merton was a Trappist Monk, theologian, and author of more than fifty books.*

Illustrated by Jennifer Tucker

WE OUGHT TO GIVE *thanks* FOR ALL FORTUNE

C.S. LEWIS

We ought to give thanks for all fortune: if it is "good," because it is good, if "bad" because it works in us patience, humility, and the contempt of this world and the hope of our eternal country.

—C. S. Lewis. This quote comes from a tweet by @CSLewisDaily, quoting a 1948 correspondence between British author C. S. Lewis and Italian priest Don Giovanni Calabria.

Illustrated by Bridget Hurley
Hand-lettered by Ann-Margret Hovsepian

Gratitude can transform common days into thanksgivings, turn routine jobs into joy, and change ordinary opportunities into blessings.

—William Arthur Ward. An editor, teacher, and pastor, Ward (1921–1994) is one of America's most quoted authors of inspirational maxims. His column "Pertinent Proverbs" was a regular feature in the Fort Worth Star-Telegram newspaper.

Illustrated by Ann-Margret Hovsepian

Shout for joy to the LORD, all the earth.

—*Psalm 100:1 (NIV)*

Illustrated by Jennifer Tucker

DON'T WORRY ABOUT ANYTHING; INSTEAD, PRAY ABOUT EVERYTHING

PHILIPPIANS 4:6

Don't worry about anything; instead, pray about everything.
Tell God what you need, and thank him for all he has done.

—*Philippians 4:6* (NLT)

Illustrated by Katie Howe
Hand-lettered by Ann-Margret Hovsepian

Choose
contentment
& thankfulness
now

JOANNA GAINES

It's up to us to choose contentment and thankfulness now—
and to stop imagining that we have to have
everything perfect before we'll be happy.

—Joanna Gaines, in The Magnolia Story *by Chip and Joanna Gaines
with Mark Dagostino (Thomas Nelson, 2016)*

Illustrated by Laura Marshall Denny

The soul that gives thanks can find comfort in everything;
the soul that complains can find comfort in nothing.

—Hannah Whitall Smith, from Living in the Sunshine (Revell, 1906). Smith (1832–1911)
was raised in a strict Quaker home. She later dedicated herself to searching the Scriptures
and in the early 1860s became a speaker and author in the Holiness movement.

Illustrated by Jennifer Tucker

Therefore let us be grateful for receiving a kingdom that cannot be shaken, and thus let us offer to God acceptable worship, with reverence and awe.

—*Hebrews 12:28* (ESV)

When you go through deep waters, I will be with you.

Isaiah 43:2

When you go through deep waters,
    I will be with you.
When you go through rivers of difficulty,
    you will not drown.
When you walk through the fire of oppression,
    you will not be burned up;
the flames will not consume you.

—Isaiah 43:2 (NLT)

Illustrated by Bridget Hurley
Hand-lettered by Ann-Margret Hovsepian

I don't have to chase extraordinary moments to find happiness—it's right in front of me if I'm paying attention and practicing gratitude.

—Brené Brown, in an interview conducted by Gretchen Rubin
for Forbes magazine, July 15, 2011

Illustrated by Ann-Margret Hovsepian

Whatever attitude we bring into a situation will be *Multiplied*

Lysa TerKeurst

Whatever attitude we bring into a situation will be multiplied.
Let's bring an attitude worth being multiplied into this day.
An attitude of hope. An attitude of love.
An attitude of humility and gratitude. An attitude of joy.

—*Lysa TerKeurst, from her tweet on January 4, 2020. TerKeurst is a* New York Times
bestselling author and president of Proverbs 31 Ministries.

Illustrated by Jennifer Tucker

Give thanks to the LORD, for he is good!

—Psalm 107:1 (NLT)

Illustrated by Radha Carlson

Rest and be thankful.

—William Wordsworth. The English poet (1770–1850) was one of the founders of Romanticism, a literary movement that prized nature and human emotion.

Illustrated by Laura Marshall Denny